INCREASE YOUR IMPACT AND INFLUENCE

With Everything from Books, Blogs, and Scripts
to Videos, Online Courses, Workshops, and Consulting

by Gini Graham Scott

INCREASE YOUR IMPACT AND INFLUENCE

Copyright © 2019 by Gini Graham Scott

All rights reserved. No part of this book may be used or reproduced by any means, graphic, electronic, or mechanical, including photocopying, recording, taping or by any information storage retrieval system without the written permission of the author except in the case of brief quotations embodied in critical articles and reviews.

TABLE OF CONTENTS

INTRODUCTION 5
   Sharing Your Message in Multiple Formats 6
   How I Developed this Approach 9
   Developing Your Own Impact and Influence Campaign 10
CHAPTER 1: THE MANY FORMATS FOR PRESENTING YOUR MATERIAL 13
   Focusing in On Your Message 14
   Redesigning and Repurposing Your Material 16
CHAPTER 2: THE DIFFERENT FORMATS TO CHOOSE FROM 19
   Blogs and Articles 19
   Social Media Copy 19
   Books 20
   Press Releases and Press Kits 23
   Website Copy 24
   Brochures and Flyers 25
   PowerPoint Presentations 26
   Videos 26
   White Papers 29
   Speeches 30
   Workshops, Seminars, Webinars, and Teleseminars 31
   Radio Shows and Podcasts 32
   Online Classes and Courses 33
   Coaching and Consulting 34
   Newsletters 34
   Query Letters to Gain Assistance or Make Sales 35
   Scripts 37
   Advertising and Promotional Copy 38
   Packaging and Presenting Your Material 39
   Delegating and Outsourcing Your Work 40
   What's Next? 43
ABOUT THE AUTHOR 45
OTHER AVAILABLE BOOKS ON INSPIRATION, MOTIVATION, AND SUCCESS 46

INTRODUCTION

Today, just about everyone wants to increase their impact and influence. This can take various forms, from gaining more credibility and authority to attaining more power and prestige. It can also occur in various ways, from gaining a steady social media following to being a widely recognized on TV appearances and podcasts. Having a book, blog, published article, video, or radio show, or being a recognized consultant at something can be a source of influencing, inspiring, and motivating others, too.

In turn, you may want this impact and influence for many reasons -- to support a cause, to gain more friends and followers, to impress your family members, to inspire and motivate others, to build your business and increase your income.

Whatever the reason, you want to attract others to you and have an impact or influence on them in some way.

Sharing Your Message in Multiple Formats

The way to do this is to share your message in multiple formats designed to reach your intended audience in the ways they prefer to get that message. This message is whatever content or communication you want to convey -- and today there are more ways than ever to spread what you want to say. As a result, you can repackage and repurpose your message in various ways in order to break through the huge clutter of chatter in today's supercharged information age. And doing so can help others hear and respond to your message.

The process of gaining influence is a little like meeting someone and getting to know them, so they "know, like, and trust you," a commonly use expression in business today. What often happens is you initially meet someone once or twice at business meetings, and you barely know who they are.

For example, I go to many business mixers or trade shows where I pick up business cards. But unless I take notes about what they are interested in and what I should do to follow-up, I generally don't even remember their name after a day or two. However, by the third and fourth time, they have become familiar, and in most cases, I am learning to like them -- unless they do something untoward, such as being overly loud and pushy. By the fifth or sixth time, their familiarity has turned to trust. After all, they keep showing up, so I have come to feel they are likely to be trustworthy.

It's much the same with your content. A single mention of a book or article by you or a single encounter with your talk or video might help to put you on someone's radar, but you are likely to hover on the border. But as a person encounters different messages from you in different formats, you move closer and closer to the center of the target. When you have a single touchpoint for your message, such as a book or video, you need the repetition of marketing, advertising, and promotion to become top of mind. But if you create multiple touchpoints, such as having a book, blog, website, and video, that can help to reinforce your message and increase your presence, so you have more influence. This can translate into different benefits depending on your goals and your audience.

For instance, if your goal is to build your business and make more money, your audience is prospective customers or clients, and you want to choose the content and platforms for sharing that content which will appeal to them, such as your website, online shopping platform, and videos. If you are promoting a cause, your audience is individuals who might become supporters and possibly politicians and legislators, and they might be best reached through a book, crowdfunding campaign, and videos. If you want to teach, inspire, and motivate individuals, your market might be those interested in self-help subjects, and they might be especially responsive to books, blogs, podcasts, and workshops.

Sharing your message in multiple formats can also help with lead generation for your business, since repurposing your content allows it to be in more places where prospective customers can find it. For instance, if you have a book, prospects can view it on Amazon. If you have multiple articles, search engines will be more likely to find you. Likewise, videos on YouTube, podcasts on iTunes, or social media posts on Facebook, Instagram, or LinkedIn will increase your visibility. The more places you are the better, because some people like to Google for information, others like to look for books, others prefer to listen to podcasts, still others like their information from videos. By sharing our message in different ways, you cast a wider net, so you increase your chances for generating leads, getting customers, and making sales.

    Thus, first hone your message, so you are clear what you want to say. Then, determine your most appropriate audience or audiences to respond to your message. Choose the type of formats in which to share your messages and adapt your message to that format. Finally, after you have presented your message in the chosen formats, market, promote, and publicize how you are expressing your message in these different ways.

    While this last phase of marketing, promotion, and publicity is an important factor in increasing your impact and influence, my focus in this book -- and in the multiple formats I will share my own message -- is on creating that message in different formats. So I will briefly talk about marketing and promotion strategies and suggest various for books, videos, courses, and other materials on this topic.

How I Developed this Approach

I developed this approach after working with several clients who wanted to slice and dice their content in different ways.

One client started five years ago with a single book in the criminal justice field -- half of it a memoir about his wife's nightmare experience with the criminal justice system, the other half a discussion of different problems with the system and how to fix them. After that there were a few more books, a website, some short videos with book highlights, press releases, software programs to get higher video rankings on Google, a series of blogs, and spinning articles to turn a single article into different versions to be published on multiple sites. Then came social media postings with insights and photos for his books, followed by informational videos, audio books, white papers with advice for law enforcement professionals and politicians, PowerPoint presentations, and videos made from these presentations. In short, I took the same basic content, starting with his book on a specific topic, and then I found different ways to repackage and repurpose the same content from different chapters.

With other clients I have started with blogs and website copy and turned that into books, videos, and other materials. The result was that these clients began getting reviews from book reviewers, invitations to appear on podcasts and radio shows, requests to do a guest blog, and invitations to join panels or speak at various events. Then those appearances led to ideas for new projects to lead to even more impact and influence.

Developing Your Own Impact and Influence Campaign

You can similarly create your campaign to gain more influence and impact regardless of your purpose and the audience you want to reach. You just have to determine your message and the different modalities or formats to use to reach your audience.

To this end, I will provide an overview of each of these formats and how to best present your message in that format. You can then decide which formats to use and the best order in which to develop them.

Say you start with blogs on your website or blogging site and post some social media photos and comments on Facebook and Instagram, which is an easy way to get started. You might then turn a half dozen blogs or a few dozen posts into a book. You might most easily start with an e-book, and then you can turn that into a paperback book, which you market it through your website and Amazon. Next might come an audiobook, and perhaps you might turn that same content into a video with photos, using a video platform. Then that might become the basis for a talk, workshop or seminar you give in person and later develop into an online webinar, which can lead to requests for you to be a consultant or coach on your topic.

In a future book, I'll describe in more detail the basics for sharing your message in each format and describe how to use that format most effectively. This overview can help you decide which are the best formats for sharing your message, then a more detailed description of that format will provide a step by step discussion of what to do. Or if you have already decided what you want to do, simply read that more detailed discussion.

In the future, I'll also discuss how to decide on an effective strategy for determining how to share your message, based on a variety of considerations which differ for everyone. That's because your choice of formats depends on a number of factors, which include your message and audience, the time you can devote to sharing your message, your budget for creating your content in different formats, and your plans and costs for marketing and promoting your message.

At some point, you may need help in working out your program, and that's where I can help with some individual coaching or consulting to guide you in creating your material and determining the best formats for presenting it. Part of this discussion can include a consideration of different marketing and promotion strategies, but for specific recommendations on what to do, you can turn to any of the many marketing and promotion gurus to guide you. You can also find many local and virtual assistants to help you set up your marketing and promotion campaign.

So now, start thinking about your content and how to present and repurpose to increase your impact and influence. Get ready, get set, and go to it! Now!

CHAPTER 1: THE MANY FORMATS FOR PRESENTING YOUR MATERIAL

Today, there are multiple ways of presenting your material in all kinds of formats and on all sorts of platforms. At one time, books, articles, and speeches were the main vehicles for presenting any kind of information.

But now, with the information explosion and new technologies, you can use many approaches and choose those ones that best work for you.

Such opportunities for choice parallel new developments in marketing, promotion, and publicity, since there are now multiple methods and channels for promoting what you are doing to different audiences. I will briefly discuss these different channels for promoting various types of content. This way you have a better idea of your choices, whether you decide to do your own marketing and promotion or look to a professional to guide you or do it for you, which I recommend.

Focusing in On Your Message

The basic idea behind selecting different formats for presenting your material is that you reorganize or restructure the same basic information, so you present it in different ways. The process is a little like branding, where you develop a consistent look and message to create certain identity, so you are known for a particular type of expertise. Your topic or field doesn't matter. The idea is to specialize so your audience understands what you are writing, saying, or otherwise presenting. This way you stay on message and on brand, so you maintain a focus that leads people to better know, like, and trust you. They come to expect certain things but not other things from you, and that is what attracts them to you.

Accordingly, the starting point for presenting your material is focusing on what your message is, and then varying it in various ways. But your core message, identity, or branding remains the same. Later, you can always expand that identity to incorporate more related topics, although if you are widely divergent in what you want to write or talk about, it may be better to set up separate identities and messages for each one. That way, you keep your focus and identity in each area, but can grow into other areas.

This process is a little like what happens in publishing or in companies with different products lines. For instance, Random House publishes a wide range of material, but it separates its content into about 45 different imprints, each with its own specialty and editorial team. Another example is cars. A company may have several lines, each under a different name, such as a more expensive luxury line, a less expensive line of family cars, a sports car line, and so on. For instance, Chevrolet has Corvettes sport cars, Silverado trucks, Suburban vans, and Malibu sedans; Toyota has its mix of Corollas, Priuses, Camrys, and other models. When you are just getting started, it's good to have just one model to focus on; then when that is successful, you can expand on the line or develop others.

Redesigning and Repurposing Your Material

Once you know your basic message, start by creating it in one way, which works best for you. For example, you might start with a blog, and once you have a few blogs, you can turn that into a book. Then, you can record that blog to turn it into a podcast, add some photos using a video platform, or turn it into a video. You can also use that copy for a PowerPoint presentation, add images, and turn it into a video. Or perhaps use that copy with photos to create a series of posts on Facebook, Instagram, or Twitter. If you don't have your own photos, you can easily get photos from free photo sites or for a few dollars from royalty free stock photo houses.

Another example is if you start with a book. You can turn the chapters into blogs and videos. You can divide the book into chapters to create shorter books. You can even make some of these permanently free or gift books, which you use to promote your other books, workshops, webinars, or online courses.

You can also publish your book in multiple formats, including a paperback, e-book, PDF, or audiobook. And a paperback or e-book can be sold through multiple channels. Amazon or Kindle are the most familiar sellers, but IngramSpark is the best outlet for library and book store sales, and Draft2Digital and Smashwords sell e-books to other outlets. Or you can distribute your e-books directly to these online sellers, such as Barnes and Noble and Kobo.

Plus there are different ways to create covers for selling your book in different formats. For instance, KDP (formerly CreateSpace) has a half-dozen templates where you just add a photo or in some cases, just your title. Or use a graphic designer to create your cover. If you do an audiobook, you need a square cover. And if you create a book as a PDF, you don't need a cover, when you offer this as a free book or for sale on your website, though you can create a cover with your own images or use a designer program with PDF templates you can modify with your own copy and images.

Additionally, you can turn certain kinds of books and other materials into scripts for short films or features. Alternatively, you can start with a logline, paragraph summary, treatment, or synopsis before writing the full-blown script.

In short, you can select a variety of formats based on taking the same material and repackaging it different ways. In this way, you can repurpose whatever you write to get "more bang for your buck" as they say. It's a little like repurposing a gift you received but can't use, so you give it to someone else who you hope will use it.

In turn, these multiple ways of repurposing your material help to build your identity and brand, since people see what you sharing in different formats that reinforce each other. Then, these multiple viewings help you become more memorable and visible, much like when a celebrity or author appears on multiple TV or radio shows promoting their latest film, show, or book. They typically say the same thing or get asked similar questions on each program, but the more they appear, the more they are familiar to the viewing audience. In sales, they typically say it takes seven pitches to make a sale, seven no's to get a yes. It's much the same in getting visibility -- you have to repeat, repeat, repeat your message, and when you use different formats and appear on different platforms, you're like the TV or radio guests who appears on multiple shows. After a while, they stand out and become familiar well-known faces. The same process will work for you.

CHAPTER 2: THE DIFFERENT FORMATS TO CHOOSE FROM

I will be discussing how to use each of the different formats in subsequent chapters. Here I want to briefly describe them, so you can see all the options. Then, you can choose which ones to use for your message.

Blogs and Articles

Blogs and articles are one of the easiest formats to get started in, since these can be short, ranging from about 500 to1500 words, and sometimes up to 2000 to 2500 words for a longer article. The main difference between blogs and articles is that blogs are typically posted on a website or blog posting service. By contrast, articles usually appear in print or online magazines. However, the content of both can be the same, and usually they have a byline, unless the article or blog is featured on your own website.

A single blog or article can easily be combined with other to form a book or other larger piece, or it can be repackaged in different formats, such as turned into a PowerPoint or video.

Social Media Copy

Social media copy is another easy way to get started, since each post is made up of short copy -- up to 280 words if posted on Twitter, and often even shorter on Instagram - typically up to 3 lines of 125 words to be seen as a post without clicking "more" to read further, though longer form copy is allowed. The other main sites for social media copy are Facebook, LinkedIn, and YouTube, though you can post on smaller niche sites, such as Reddit, too.

Social media posts are good for taking highlights from other material -- or if you start off with this copy, you can combine several posts into a larger blog or article. Once you have enough of them, you can use that to create a book, which I did from both Facebook and Instagram posts.

In the case of Facebook, I wrote three books, taking posts I wrote on techniques for conducting a social media campaign and self-publishing to publish these titles, each consisting of the social media copy plus the photo that appeared with it: *Conducting a Monthly Social Media Campaign on Four Major Platforms, Conducting a Monthly Social Media Video Campaign,* and *The Self-Publishing Solution: Tips You Can Use for Success from a 12-Week Social Media Campaign.*

For Instagram, I created four books, each on a success, self-help, or motivational theme: *Control Your Thoughts, Control Your Life: 60 Ways to Make Every Day Even Better, Pursue Your Passion: 60 Ways to Follow Your Passion; Work It Right: 60 Ways to Gain More Success at Work,* and *Find True Happiness: 60 Ways to Discover What Makes You Happy.* Each book included the additional subtitle: *Based on 60 Posts on Instagram.*

Likewise, you can turn a series of social media posts into something else, particularly if these posts are organized around a particular theme.

Books

Today books can be very short, even pamphlet or booklet size, since people tend to read less and like their material in smaller chunks. By contrast, traditional books have averaged 250 to 350 pages, and some still are that long.

Whatever the length, a book is an ideal format to gain credibility, visibility, and authority, since you can point to something tangible you have written. One way that some people get started with a book is writing a chapter in an anthology, which is like turning an article or blog into a chapter. Such chapters are typically about 10 to 15 pages -- about 2500 to 4000 words.

But rather than have a chapter that can get lost in a compilation book with other authors, you can easily turn that chapter into a book of at least 24 pages. And to lengthen the book, you can always use larger type or add illustrations. Generally it is best to create your own stand-alone book, so you stand out as a published book author, rather than someone in a chapter in a book featuring a dozen or more authors with their own chapters, though sometimes this combination publication can help you stand out through joint publicity.

Any book can be published in multiple formats which include:
- print books, such as published as a print-on-demand (POD) book by KDP in paperback or by IngramSpark in paperback or hardcover editions; these can also be printed in long runs by a regular publisher;
- e-books, such as published as a mobi file on Kindle or as an e-book on other platforms such as by the aggregators: Draft2Digital and Smashword. Also, you can provide them direct to online booksellers, such as Barnes and Noble or Kobo;
- audiobooks, which you can narrate yourself, hire a narrator, or use a text to voice software program;

- a PDF, which you can sell from your website or use as a gift book to promote other books or services you offer; and you can additionally create an attractive cover for the PDF or just have a regular title page;
- mini-books, in which you take am introduction and one or two chapters, plus your contact information, in order to introduce people to a longer book or to your products or services; often these books are offered in various formats for free or at a very low price, such as .99c for an e-book which costs you practically nothing and $5.95 for a print book, where you have to factor in printing costs.

- a combination of formats, which include mini-books, permafree books, gift books, illustrated books with your own or stock photos, and nutshell books, which include short excerpts from other books you have written.

Additionally, you can set up online books with links to your website, to an online site that sells your book, and to other products and services of your own or which you are selling for others.

Press Releases and Press Kits

Once you have your message in other formats, such as a book, blog series, or social media campaign, you can promote this with a press release for the media. Or write your press release in the form of a letter to an editor or to a host or producer for a podcast or radio show. Later you can follow up with a phone call, if appropriate. Normally its best to start with a written communication and later follow up, though sometimes an initial call and then follow-up letter or release works well.

The purpose of the press release or letter to the media is to summarize whatever you are doing in a captivating way, so the print media will publish your material or contact you for an interview for an article, while the broadcast media will invite you to be a guest. Normally, it's best to start locally and build on that to expand your reach to the national press.

While you can usually send these releases or letters by email, you can also post them on your website, ideally on a media page.

A press kit expands upon a press release by including other material, such as a list of questions to ask you in an interview; one or more photos of you, your book, your product, or service; an article or two by you; a list of media appearances; a list of testimonials' sample chapters from your book; and more. The particular items to include depend on what you have already done. Later, you can add to or change the contents of your press kit as you do more to share your message.

Website Copy

Virtually everyone needs a website or even multiple websites if you have multiple messages for different audiences. While a basic website can be a few pages to give you a presence and highlight your message, as you do more, add more pages with more information about what you are doing. These additional pages increase your credibility and findability -- your likelihood to turn up in searches, because you have more information about yourself.

Also, use your website to provide samples of whatever you are doing, such as a chapter in a book, some articles, links to your videos, press releases, clips of radio shows or podcasts, and order forms for whatever you are selling.

In other words, don't just use your website to tell what you do, but show this by presenting the many ways you share your message.

Brochures and Flyers

In you have something to promote or sell, brochures and flyers are good for presenting the key points of your message, often in bullet points. If you have something to sell, add an order form or link to make a purchase.

Typically, these brochures and flyers are used to hand out to people at events or trade shows. But you can also post the content online -- either on a web page or as a downloadable PDF.

PowerPoint Presentations

PowerPoint presentations are an ideal way of sharing your message to groups and organizations, or use them for an online course. You can develop the content from your books or articles, or you can first create the presentation and turn that into a book, article or video.

Ideally, keep the content on each slide short -- perhaps up to 4-7 bullet points. Then, for added interest, add a photo or two on each slide.

Besides using PowerPoints for in-person presentations, you can post them on your website or on a LinkedIn SlideShare site, which features millions of presentations in several dozen content categories. It is one of the top 100 sites visited in the world, so this is a great way to get even more visibility.

Videos

While you can have a videographer create a video for you, you can also create a video from your own content. It's easy to do using one of the many video platforms available, where you add your text and images, or you can turn a PowerPoint presentation into a video.

You can easily render any presentation into a video using a Camtasia Add On, where you just click a few buttons and a few minutes later you have an mp4 video.

You can additionally create a voice-over audio track where you click from slide to slide as you speak. Or you can create .JPG images from each PowerPoint slide, place them on a track in Camtasia or other editing program, and add a voice-over or music to that. You don't even have to do the voice-over yourself, since you can use text-to-voice technology and a choice of computer generated voices to turn your text into an audio file. Then, you match the audio of your written text to the images or text in your video. If you already have a completed video, you can add the voice-over or music to that.

Once you have a completed video, thou can put it on YouTube, Vimeo, on your website, on social media sites, or share it in other ways. The key is having your content in a video format, so those who prefer viewing videos to reading the printed word will get your message. Also, a video will reinforce any other way they have gotten your message, such as from an article, blog, or radio interview.

Such videos can, in turn, take various forms. These can be short promotional videos of about 10-20 seconds, informational videos of about 30-120 seconds, or documentaries of several minutes. If you have enough time on the video, you can combine your message with video comments from others, or even add background shots for more visual variety.

You can do anything in creating these videos from making stand-alone videos to creating a series on different topics, which I did this for one of my clients for whom I created 120 promotional and informational videos. Additionally, I turned eight white papers developed from eight chapters in one of his books into a series of 20 five to seven minute videos with information about different criminal justice problems followed by suggestions and recommendations on what to do to fix what was wrong. I first created a PowerPoint presentation with bullet points for each video, added one or two photos for each slide, and turned that into a video with a voice-over. I animated each slide so each point on it appeared one after another to make the presentation even more dramatic.

White Papers

The white paper is good format if you have a serious message and want to propose a resolution or action steps, such as if you are writing about science, technology, social issues, or political trends. You present your message with a discussion of the problem or issue followed by a section with your recommendations or suggestions on what to do about the situation.

Typically, white papers are about 5 to 15 pages. Often you can create such a paper from something you have already written -- such as from a chapter in a book or from a series of articles, blogs, or speeches. Then, for even more impact, you can turn a white paper into a PowerPoint Presentation or video, as described above.

Speeches

      A good way to get known is to give talks about what you do and how you can help others, usually by speaking free and locally to get started. While you can talk off the cuff, it helps to have a prepared speech and you can use a PowerPoint presentation or video to supplement what you say.
      If you already have a book, articles, blogs or other material, you can draw on these to create your speech, though you might add some personal touches to increase your rapport with your audience. Alternatively, you can create your speech first and turn that into an article, blog, book, or other material.
      Speeches can be a way to sell products and services after your talk, as well as get clients. Thus, having brochures, flyers, or postcards with links to your website can help you further connect with your audience after your talk.

Workshops, Seminars, Webinars, and Teleseminars

Workshops, seminars, webinars, and teleseminars are another way to repackage your content. You can easily combine any one of these with book sales, videos, and other materials.

A seminar is more like giving a longer speech and combining it with some Q&A or some audience interaction -- usually for a 1-2 hour period.

A workshop might begin with a talk by you, but it commonly features hands-on participation by attendees. An example is when you give a 20 to 30 minute opening presentation and then involve participants in a series of activities, such as sharing with one another, designing a product or service based on tips from your talk, or writing down ideas for a later discussion.

Commonly, workshops and seminars are presented in-person, though some are presented online and include viewer questions and comments via written chats or video input, using a platform like Zoom.

A webinar is essentially a seminar on a topic presented through online conferencing, such as on Zoom or GotoWebinar. Usually it features about 30-60 minutes of presentation, often presented with a PowerPoint or video created from PowerPoint slides. Most include a video or audio of the presenter speaking to the participants, followed by 10 to 15 minutes of questions from participants using the chat function or speaking through a live video stream.

A teleseminar is a seminar conducted on the phone, although these have largely been replaced by webinars. I have found very few presentations by the phone only now that video platforms have become very common.

Radio Shows and Podcasts

Radio talk shows and podcasts are another way to get out your message, whether on your own show or as a guest on someone else's show. Whatever the format, use the show to showcase the main points of your message. You can get a free hosting service for your show on sites like blogtalkradio.com where you have to do most of the promotion or sign-up for a sponsored show on other platforms which do more promotion for you.

If it's your own program, you might use talking points from your articles, blogs, books, or videos to discuss the topic and invite callers to comment. Or you might have a guest respond to your ideas and engage in a debate. Your show is also a good way to pitch information on your book, products, or services at the end and during ad breaks every 10 to 15 minutes or so, unless you are using these ads for sponsors who are helping to fund your program.

If you have a guest appearance, be prepared to discuss the main points in your message. To get on the show, you usually need to send a press release or email query to the program host or producer. To help guide the discussion, include a list of questions to ask you. You can include in your press kit or send them to the host or producer before your appearance. At the end and sometimes during the program, the host will usually invite you to give out information about your website and your book, products, or services.

Online Classes and Courses

In recent years, online classes and courses have become increasingly popular. For many people this is an alternative to reading books -- or a class can be combined with reading print, e-books, or PDFs with additional information. While some classes feature an on-camera presenter, most classes feature videos made from PowerPoint slides, with multiple classes organized into modules on a topic, much like having chapters in a book. Sometimes classes mix-in videos with the presenter speaking to the camera.

In some cases, you can develop your class by recording chapters in a book or reading from articles or blogs. Alternatively, after you create your class, you can turn that material into a book or a series of articles and blogs. Typically, classes are about 6-15 minutes for each recording, though some can run a little longer to 20 to 30 minutes, and occasionally as long as 60 to 90 minutes. On average, 3-7 classes make up a module.

You put your classes together by creating an outline where you decide how to divide up your message into sections or parts. Then, you decide on how many topics or classes to include in each module. After your classes are recorded and turned into a video, you can share your course on various platforms, such as Teachable, Udemy, and Thinkific. You also determine what to charge for it, depending the number and length of classes, the subject matter, how well you are known, and comparable prices for that type of course.

Consulting and Coaching

In certain fields, you might want to or consulting or coaching, and any of the other formats you use can be a lead-in for this. For example, in your book, on your website, at the end of your article, or in a video, webinar, workshop, or seminar, you might invite people to sign-up for consulting on a particular issue facing them. Or you might offer to coach them with ongoing online or in-person guidance on a project they are doing.

Sometimes coaching and consulting can lead people to want to read your books, sign up for your courses, or otherwise seek out further information from you. However, more typically, someone will seek you out for coaching and consulting after they have received your message in one of more formats and then they want to learn more from you.

Commonly, consulting is designed to help with a particular problem, where you provide one or two hours of input. By contrast, coaching is more of a long-term commitment, where someone hires you to advise and guide them for a month or two to help them not only overcome a particular problem but give them ongoing recommendations to improve their business, work, or life. For instance, there are life coaches, executive coaches, writing coaches, business coaches, you name it. More and more people are hiring coaches to act as mentors they can look to for guidance in many different areas of their life.

Newsletters

Newsletters are still another way to share your message on an ongoing basis with individuals who are on your mailing list or you hope will join it. You can also use newsletters as an incentive when you send an email, place an ad, or invite website visitors to sign up for more information or free gift from you.

A newsletter is typically a weekly or occasional collection of comments, short articles, announcements, helpful tips, and photos. It can include excerpts from your books, articles, and blogs; your thoughts about current events; ideas you might later use in your books, articles, and blogs, and announcements about what you are doing. Other possibilities are offers to participate in workshops and seminars, information about your consulting and coaching programs, clips from articles others have written about you, tips on how readers can improve their life or business; and more. You can also include guest articles and announcements about their events and sales offerings, especially if they are an affiliate who is offering you a commission (commonly 10-20%) for any sign-ups or purchases.

If you have the time and commitment or an assistant who can help you do this, a regular newsletter is a great way to establish an ongoing dialogue with individuals who may become customers for additional products and services. It also offers a great way that others can readily share information about you with others.

Query Letters to Gain Assistance or Make Sales

Targeted query letter can be another important way to spread your message or pitch your products or services to those who receive your letter or pass it on to others in their organization. While these are one and one messages to a particular individual, you don't have to send them individually, since you can obtain software for personalizing these messages so they look like they come from your email, such as Group Mail Plus. Platforms like MailChimp, Get Response and AWeber can send out these personalized emails, too. A service like PublishersAgentsFilms (www.publishersagentsfilms.com) can send out these emails for you to its own database of contacts in different industries.

Some of the common reasons for sending a query letter are these:
- to contact agents or publishers about a proposed or completed book,
- to contact film producers, film agents, distributors, or sales agents about a script or film project,
- to contact legislators or politicians about your recommended approach to resolving a social problem or your ideas for new legislation,
- to contact the owner, manager, or CEO of a company about a job opportunity
- to contact potential investors or venture capitalists about a proposed business

And so on. You get the idea. In a query letter, you boil down your message into a short subject line of about 10-15 words, follow that with a sentence or two summarizing your message, and add another paragraph or two about your project, product, service, or yourself. Finally, you offer to send the recipient, if interested, more information. After that, you hope the recipient will want to follow up, and if so, you continue the conversation from there.

Scripts

If you are creating a video to showcase you or your work, you need a script or at least an outline of what scenes to include. You can either prepare your copy from scratch or adapt it from something else. For example, if you are turning a PowerPoint into a video, the copy becomes your script. Then, you build on that with visuals, such as photos or video clips, and you decide whether the written copy should be spoken or not. You might add in some music, too.

You also need scripts for promotional and informational videos, and then use that as a guide for adding images, video clips, and any music or voice-over.

Where possible, adapt the copy you have written for other purposes into your script.

Should you be inspired to write an original script with dialog, the most commonly use software is Final Draft, which will guide you in writing up the action, characters, dialog, and other elements to create a finished script ready for production. You can also create a logline, paragraph summary, treatment, and a synopsis for pitching your script to potential producers and investors.

Advertising and Promotional Copy

Your advertising and promotional copy is especially important for helping you make an impact, whatever you want promote or sell. I'll just touch on this briefly, since this book is focused on your content, and this copy is part of your marketing campaign.

Just keep in mind that any advertising and promotion you do should be consistent with your brand identity. You also need to test out different copy and strategies until you have an approach that works -- then repeat and expand it. For example, if you have a successful Facebook ad, besides running it again, consider increasing your budget and post that ad more widely, or consider advertising for different markets. Perhaps run the ad on different platforms, such as Google or Instagram.

Other places to advertise and promote your product or service include online sales sites, such as Shopify and ClickBank, if you have products that appeal to their markets. Shopify is ideal for popular consumer items, like jewelry, clothing, games, and toys, while ClickBank is ideal for popular how-to and self-help topics, ideas for making or saving money, and help with running a small business.

Packaging and Presenting Your Material

You can dress up your book covers and sales material in a number of ways to best package and present your material. There are multiple programs you can use, such as graphics software or online services with templates for your copy and images. If you don't have the skills, you can get help from local designers and gig workers on sites like Fiverr and Upwork. Another possibility for outsourcing are companies with a team of designers, such as 99Designs, which I used several times to create book covers for one of my clients.

Ideally, draw on your already written material for copy and image ideas. That will both suggest ideas and help you come up with phrases or images that reinforce your brand identity, while giving your work a more professional finished look.

For example, don't just provide a PDF with a title page. Instead, add a cover with an attractively designed illustration that looks like a regular book cover. Or if you have digital products that you stream to buyers or offer as a CD or file download, create a cover for the program, as if it is a physical product, and create ad copy that displays this. An example of this approach is several software programs I have gotten with templates for creating videos and audio programs. Although I get them by downloading files or accessing files online, the ad shows a box with an attractive cover and a display of CDs with the same attractive design spread out like a fan. I won't receive any CDs since I'm purchasing a digital product I can access or download online. But the illustration makes whatever I'm getting seem more tangible and real.

Delegating and Outsourcing Your Work

Delegating and outsourcing your work can be another way of expanding your reach, and thereby increasing your impact and influence. You can work with employees and assistants both locally and virtually.

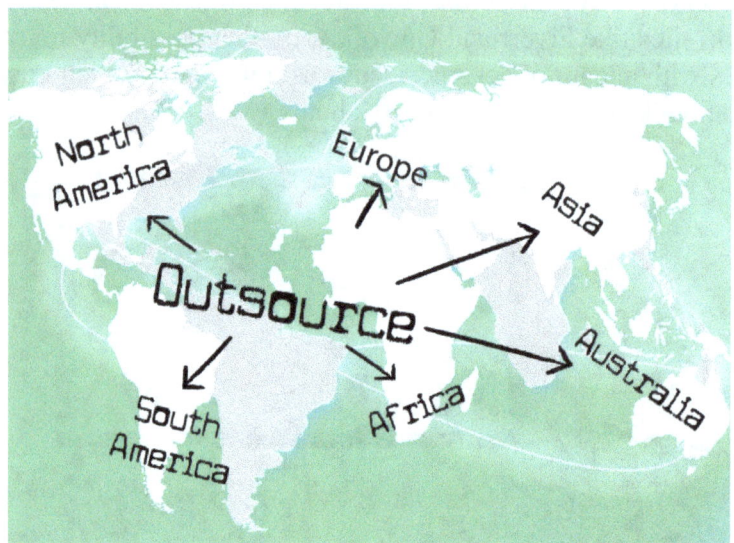

Often it can help you guide and direct those working for you if you create a written manual for them. This manual might include excerpts from things you have written, along with guidelines on what to do or say in particular situations. You can also include scripted questions and responses along with steps to follow to carry out particular tasks. At some point this manual could even be turned into a blog, article, or book with tips for others, thereby turning these guidelines for your employees or assistants into one more saleable product.

Today, the terms "delegating" and "outsourcing" are often used interchangeably, though you might think of delegating as taking tasks you might normally do and hiring someone else to do it. For example, instead of doing the Internet research or compiling a database yourself, you might hire an assistant to do this for you as an employee or independent contractor.

Legally, there are a number of guidelines for whether a person you hire is considered an employee or an independent contractor, so if in doubt, check what is the common practice for your area and industry. But generally, a person is considered an employee and subject to the laws governing employees if they work for you on a regular basis for a certain number of hours, are instructed to do the work a certain way, and are subject to careful supervision. By contrast, a person might be considered an independent contractor if they can choose their own hours, particularly if they work part-time on a sporadic and occasional basis, are only given general instructions about what to do, and are not closely supervised. Also, a person is more likely to be considered an independent contractor if they have other people they work for besides you. Ideally, when you are just starting to build your impact, it's best to hire those working for you as independent contractors, since you will have more flexibility. You also don't have to worry about various employee requirements, such as workers' comp insurance and health benefits.

As for outsourcing, which might be considered a form of delegating, you are hiring outside services, which might be local or based anywhere, to assist you with various tasks, and usually these are individuals or companies that specialize in a particular type of service. For instance, if you are running a social media campaign, a virtual assistant or VA can help you with the posts and follow-up. If you are doing an email marketing campaign, they can help by sending emails and responding to those who express interest in learning more. If you are advertising on Facebook, Amazon, Google, or elsewhere, they can help by placing ads. Some of these services can help by writing the copy for you, or you can write it yourself. Then, too, you might hire a publicist or marketing assistant to handle your publicity or marketing.

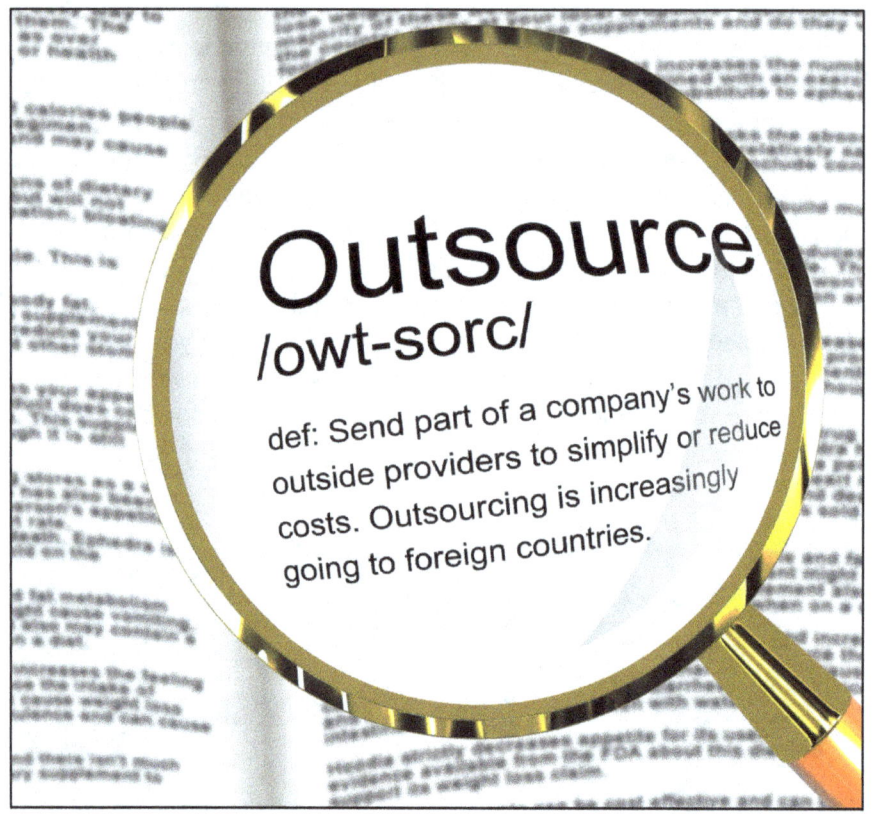

  In all of these cases of delegating or outsourcing, you can write your copy yourself or turn it over to others.
  But however you work out the details of what the content should be, it's a good idea to create written guidelines or a manual describing exactly what you want the employee, independent contractor, or VA to do. This way, you have clearly outlined what you want, and you can give someone your step-by-step plan for what to do, and you don't have to spend as much time going over the instructions for what you want done. You might need to provide a short overview in person, over the phone, on online, or via email, and you may need to be available to answer questions. However, your guidelines should help to make it very clear what you want. Consider creating them like writing a procedures or protocol manual for the assistants who work for you.

What's Next?

Now you have an overview of the many different ways to increase your impact and influence. You can choose among them and prioritize what you want to do when.

In other books, I'll discuss in more detail how to use different formats, drawing on my experience and that of others.

For now, think about what you want your message to be and consider the audience or audiences to target. It's best to begin with a single message and focus on targeting that. Then, after this is launched successfully, you can think about other messages and markets.

Once you are clear on your message and audience(s), think about the best ways to reach them. Then, pick out a few formats to start with Perhaps make a list of the different things you want to do and prioritize them by the order in which to do them. After that, you can read in more depth about using a particular approach.

So now get started, and may you impact and influence more people than ever, whatever the message you want to share.

ABOUT THE AUTHOR

GINI GRAHAM SCOTT, Ph.D., J.D., is a nationally known writer, consultant, speaker, and seminar leader, specializing in business and work relationships, professional and personal development, social trends, and popular culture. She has published 50 books with major publishers. She has worked with dozens of clients on memoirs, self-help, popular business books, and film scripts. Writing samples are at www.changemakerspublishingandwriting.com.

She is the founder of Changemakers Publishing, featuring books on work, business, psychology, social trends, and self-help. The company has published over 150 print, e-books, and audiobooks. She has licensed several dozen books for foreign sales, including the UK, Russia, Korea, Spain, and Japan.

She has received national media exposure for her books, including appearances on *Good Morning America, Oprah,* and *CNN.* She has been the producer and host of a talk show series, *Changemakers*, featuring interviews on social trends.

Scott is active in a number of community and business groups, including the Lafayette, Pleasant Hill, and Walnut Creek Chambers of Commerce. She is a graduate of the prestigious Leadership Contra Costa program. She does workshops and seminars on the topics of her books.

She is also the writer and executive producer of 10 films in distribution, release, or production. Her most recent films that have been released include *Driver, The New Age of Aging,* and *Infidelity.*

She received her Ph.D. from the University of California, Berkeley, and her J.D. from the University of San Francisco Law School. She has received five MAs at Cal State University, East Bay, most recently in Communication.

OTHER AVAILABLE BOOKS ON INSPIRATION, MOTIVATION, AND SUCCESS

Control Your Life, Control Your Thoughts
Pursue Your Passion
Work It Right
The Courage Book
The Gratitude Book
The Anger Book
The Forgiveness Book
The Vision Board Book
Affirming Your Success
Animal Insights
The Animal Experience
20 Rhymes for Your Success
Turn Your Dreams into Reality
The Wisdom of Water: To Your Success
The Wisdom of Water: Insights from Nature for Everyday Life
Mind Power: Picture Your Way to Success in Business
The Empowered Mind: How to Harness the Creative Force Within

CHANGEMAKERS PUBLISHING
3527 Mt. Diablo Blvd., #273
Lafayette, CA 94549
changemakers@pacbell.net . (925) 385-0608
www.changemakerspublishingandwriting.com